55477 EN
Ireland

Italia, Bob
ATOS BL 5.5
Points: 0.5

LG

BATTLE GROUND ACADEMY
Franklin, TN

The Countries
Ireland

Bob Italia
ABDO Publishing Company

BATTLE GROUND ACADEMY
Franklin, TN

visit us at
www.abdopub.com

Published by ABDO Publishing Company, 4940 Viking Drive, Edina, Minnesota 55435.
Copyright © 2001 by Abdo Consulting Group, Inc. International copyrights reserved in
all countries. No part of this book may be reproduced in any form without written
permission from the publisher.

Printed in the United States.

Interior Photo Credits: Corbis

Contributing Editors: Tamara L. Britton, Kate A. Furlong, and Christine Fournier
Art Direction & Maps: Neil Klinepier

Library of Congress Cataloging-in-Publication Data

Italia, Bob, 1955-
  Ireland / Bob Italia.
     p. cm. -- (The countries)
  Includes index.
  ISBN 1-57765-496-X
    1. Ireland--Juvenile literature. [1. Ireland.] I. Title. II. Series.

DA906 .I83 2001
941.5--dc21

                          2001016124

Contents

Dia duit! 4

Fast Facts 6

Timeline 7

History 8

The Emerald Isle 12

Plants & Animals 16

The Irish People 18

Economy 22

Cities.. 24

Transportation 26

Government 28

Holidays & Festivals 32

Sports & Leisure 34

Glossary 38

Web Sites.. 39

Index 40

4 *Ireland*

Dia duit!

Hello from Ireland! Ireland is an island in northwestern Europe. Ireland is known as the Emerald Isle because of its beautiful, green countryside.

Ireland's earliest settlers arrived around 7,000 B.C. from northern Great Britain. Many different groups invaded Ireland. Eventually, it was ruled by England. The country finally achieved independence in 1948.

Today, the Irish republic is a **parliamentary democracy**. It has a president and prime minister. Parliament makes its laws.

Agriculture and manufacturing are important to Ireland's **economy**. Ireland makes electrical goods, processed foods, and beer.

The Irish also have a rich literary and artistic **heritage**. Folk songs, dances, and traditional storytelling help preserve Ireland's way of life.

Dia duit! **5**

Dia duit *from Ireland!*

Ireland

Fast Facts

OFFICIAL NAME: Ireland (Eire)
CAPITAL: Dublin

LAND
- Mountain Ranges: Magillycuddy's Reeks, Donegal Mountains, Mountains of Mayo, Mountains of Connemara, Wicklow Mountains
- Highest Peak: Carrauntoohill 3,414 feet (1,041 m)
- Longest River: River Shannon 240 miles (386 km)
- Lakes: Lough Neah, Lough Corrib

PEOPLE
- Population: 3,797,257 (2000 est.)
- Major Cities: Dublin, Cork
- Official Languages: English and Gaelic
- Religion: Roman Catholic, Protestant

GOVERNMENT
- Form: Parliamentary Democracy
- Head of State: President
- Head of Government: Prime minister
- Legislature: Seanad (upper chamber), Dáil (lower chamber)
- National Anthem: "The Soldier's Song"
- Flag: One white bar flanked by one green bar and one orange bar
- Independence: 1921

ECONOMY
- Agricultural Products: Barley, beef and dairy cattle, hogs, horses, potatoes, poultry, sheep, sugar beets, wheat
- Manufactured Products: Alcoholic beverages, chemicals, clothing, computers, machinery, medicines, metal products, paper, printed materials, processed foods, textiles
- Money: One Irish pound equals 100 pence. In 2002, Ireland will begin using the euro.

Ireland's flag

Timeline

7000 B.C.	First settlers come to Ireland
300s B.C.	Celtic tribes invade Ireland
A.D. 400s	Saint Patrick brings Christianity to Ireland
1169	Norman invasion
1801	Ireland becomes part of the United Kingdom of Great Britain and Ireland
1845–1848	Famine kills about 1.5 million people
1916	Easter Rising against British rule erupts in Dublin
1921	Ireland becomes a dominion called the Irish Free State
1948	Ireland declares itself a republic
1998	Ireland and Northern Ireland sign peace agreement

Ireland's money is called the pound (L). It is divided into 100 pence. Bills are issued in 5, 10, 20, and 50 pounds. Coins come in 1, 2, 5, 10, 20, and 50 pence. There is also a 1 pound coin. In 2002, Ireland will begin using the euro (R).

History

Ireland's earliest settlers arrived in about 7,000 B.C. They traveled from northern Great Britain. Many invaders came to Ireland. The Celts, who arrived as early as the 300s B.C., were the main group. Saint Patrick spread Christianity throughout Ireland in the A.D. 400s.

The Normans invaded Ireland in 1169. Over the next 700 years, England ruled Ireland. During this time, the Irish rebelled against England's monarchs. But England continued to oppress the Irish people.

In 1801, the British and Irish **parliaments** passed the Act of Union. It made Ireland an official part of the **United Kingdom**. The Irish Parliament was then ended. Ireland sent representatives to the British Parliament.

During the early 1800s, Ireland's population grew rapidly. Most of the people lived as tenants on small farms. These poor farmers depended on potatoes for their food. From 1845 to 1848, Ireland's potato crop failed due to a plant disease. Almost 1.5 million people died of starvation or illness. More than 1 million left the country.

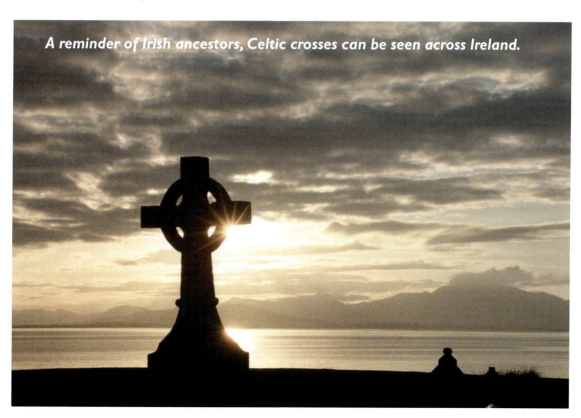

A reminder of Irish ancestors, Celtic crosses can be seen across Ireland.

Ireland's modern government began with a protest called the Easter Rising of 1916. Twenty-six counties became the Irish Free State in 1921. But six northern counties remained under British rule. These counties became Northern Ireland. Some people who wanted independence stayed in Northern Ireland. This caused people to protest with violence.

The Irish Free State adopted a written constitution in 1937. It formally declared itself the Irish Republic in 1948.

In 1985, the **United Kingdom** and Ireland signed a pact called the Anglo-Irish Agreement. It allowed Northern Ireland to remain part of the United Kingdom, as long as a majority of its citizens so desired.

In the 1980s, Ireland's **economy** struggled with high unemployment. But with growth in the technology industry, Ireland's economy has become strong.

In 1998, Northern Ireland approved a peace settlement with the Irish Republic. But tensions and violence remain between the north and the south to this day.

History **11**

O'Connel Street's many statues honor those who fought in the Easter Rising of 1916.

The Emerald Isle

The Republic of Ireland occupies most of the island of Ireland. Northern Ireland lies to the northeast. It occupies the rest of the island.

Central Ireland is mainly lowlands. The lowlands are surrounded by mountainous coasts. The central lowlands include some wooded areas, but consist mostly of gently rolling farmlands. They also include **peat bogs**.

All around the farmlands are mountains. The Donegal Mountains are in the northwest. The Mountains of Mayo and the Mountains of Connemara are in the west. Magillycuddy's Reeks are in the southwest, and the Wicklow Mountains are in the east. Ireland's highest peak is Carrauntoohill in Magillycuddy's Reeks. It is 3,414 feet (1,041 m) tall.

The Emerald Isle 13

Ireland's west coast has many beautiful features. Many inlets and bays cut into the west coast of Ireland. Hundreds of small islands also lie off the west coast. In addition, most of Ireland's lakes lie in the west.

Ireland has a mild, wet climate. Westerly winds keep the temperatures even in the summer and winter. The ocean winds also bring much rain to Ireland. The heaviest rains fall in the mountains along the west coast.

Mountains of Ireland's west coast

The Emerald Isle 15

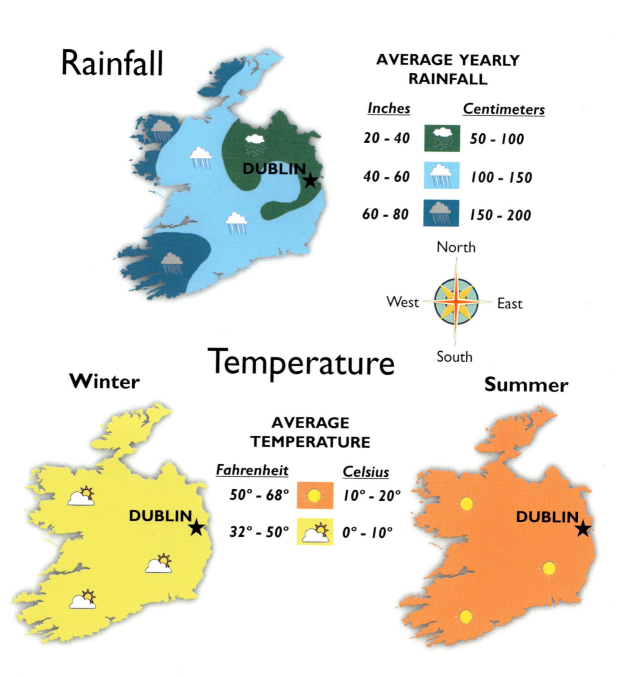

Plants & Animals

Ireland has many grasses because of its mild, moist air. But there are few trees. At one time, woodlands of the midlands had large oak forests. They were cleared over most of the country by the 1600s. Today, they are found only in remote areas.

Ireland has about 25 kinds of mammals. These include the fallow deer, red deer, badger, otter, goat, and red fox. Rabbit and other rodents live in Ireland as well. The hare and **stoat** are native to the country.

The only reptiles in Ireland are small lizards. There are no snakes. Ireland's amphibians are the newt, the frog, and the toad. The rivers and lakes have salmon, trout, char, pollan, perch, pike, and eels. Ireland has 380 kinds of wild birds. Some of Ireland's birds include swans, geese, ducks, pheasants, merlins, and falcons.

Plants & Animals 17

A female duck floats in the Lee River.

The Irish People

Over thousands of years, groups such as the Celts, Vikings, Normans, and English have all contributed to the Irish population. The Celts left behind their language. Today, it is the national language of Ireland. It is called Irish or Gaelic. English is the second official language. Most Irish people speak English.

Ireland's **constitution** allows people to practice whichever religion they choose. The majority of people in Ireland are Catholic or Protestant. Almost every Irish city has a Catholic cathedral or church. Most people attend church regularly.

Irish law requires children from the ages of 6 to 15 to go to school. Ireland's government provides funds to support the schools. Most children attend school for free. Nearly all of Ireland's schools are controlled by private organizations, mainly the Roman Catholic Church.

The Irish People 19

Girls and boys wear uniforms at a private school in Ireland.

Children attend primary school until they are 12 or 13 years old. Then they go on to secondary school until they are 17 or 18.

Most Irish people live in houses with two or three people. More and more people live in or near big cities, like Dublin. Many people work in production industries, services, education, and health. Ireland's **economy** is growing stronger each year.

Irish cooking is simple. The most popular foods include beef, **mutton**, bread, fruit, sausage, pork, smoked salmon, potatoes, and other vegetables. Potatoes grow well in Ireland's climate. They have been an important food in Ireland for hundreds of years.

One of Ireland's most famous dishes is Irish stew. It is made by boiling potatoes, onions, and pieces of mutton in a covered pot. Most Irish people enjoy drinking a glass of beer or ale with their evening meal.

The Irish People

Irish Soda Bread

4 cups whole wheat flour
1 cup bread flour
1/3 cup rolled oats
1 tsp baking soda
1 tsp salt
2 1/2 cups buttermilk

Preheat oven to 425 degrees Fahrenheit. Lightly grease two baking sheets. In large bowl, stir together whole wheat flour, white flour, rolled oats, baking soda, and salt. Mix in the buttermilk until a soft dough is formed. Knead very lightly. Divide dough into four pieces and form into rounded flat loaves. Place loaves onto prepared baking sheets. Bake until golden brown, about 30 to 45 minutes.

AN IMPORTANT NOTE TO THE CHEF: Always have an adult help with the preparation and cooking of food. Never use kitchen utensils or appliances without adult permission and supervision.

LANGUAGE

English	Gaelic
Yes	Tha
No	Níl
Thank You	Go raibh maith agat
Please	Le do thoil
Hello	Dia duit
Goodbye	Slán

Economy

Tourism and services make up the largest part of Ireland's **economy**. Industry is the second-largest part of the economy. Many world-leading companies are now located in Ireland. These companies make food products, chemicals, electronics, **pharmaceuticals**, beer, and textiles.

Agriculture is also a large part of the Irish economy. Raising cattle and dairy farming are the most important parts of the agricultural industry. The main crops are barley, wheat, sugar beets, potatoes, and oats.

Ireland has few mineral deposits. But important discoveries of lead and zinc have created a small mining industry. Ireland imports almost all of its oil for energy. But **peat** is also widely used as a fuel.

The Irish communications are based on television, radio, and newspapers. The government operates two

Economy 23

television channels and five radio stations. Every owner of a television set pays a license fee each year. There are three daily national newspapers. They include *The Irish Times*, the *Examiner*, and the *Irish Independent*. All of them are in English.

A farmer gathers peat to use as fuel.

Cities

The capital and largest city of Ireland is Dublin. It serves as the political, economic, and **cultural** center of Ireland.

Trade has always been one of Dublin's most important activities. Dublin is Ireland's largest port and major exporter. It is also the largest manufacturing city in Ireland. The city's most famous business is the Guinness Brewery. It was founded in 1759. It makes one of the world's most popular beers.

Ireland's second-largest city is Cork. It is on the River Lee in southeastern Ireland. The center of the old city is an island in the Lee. Cork is a major port. **Distilling**, **brewing**, textile making, shipbuilding, and automobile production are its major industries. And for many years, its butter market has been famous.

Dublin's Grafton Street is lined with merchants.

Transportation

Because of the large rural population, transportation in Ireland is mainly by road. There are more than 57,000 miles (92, 500 km) of roads. In Ireland, people drive on the left side of the road. Their road signs are in both Irish and English.

There are also public bus and freight services. The railway system has more than 1,200 miles (1,947 km) of track. Irish Rail transports passengers from Dublin to most large cities and towns.

Many of the goods and passenger traffic go by sea. The principal ports are on the east and south coasts. **Ferries** take passengers, goods, and road vehicles between main British and Irish ports.

Most tourists travel to Ireland by air. The main international airports are at Dublin, Belfast, Knock, Shannon, and Cork. The national airline is Aer Lingus.

Transportation 27

A farmer's herd of sheep block a road in Dooagh Village, Ireland.

Government

The Republic of Ireland is a **parliamentary democracy**. It has a president, a prime minister, and a parliament. The government is based on the **Constitution** of 1937.

The president is Ireland's official head of state. The Irish people elect the president. The president's duties include calling Parliament into session, appointing the prime minister and other officials, and signing laws passed by Parliament.

The prime minister is the real head of the government. He or she forms government policy. The prime minister also chooses a group of 7 to 15 people to advise him. They head government departments.

Opposite page: The Irish Republic's parliament meets at the Leinster House.

Government

The Irish **parliament** has two branches. The larger branch is called the Dáil Éireann. It makes Ireland's laws. The people elect 166 members to the Dáil. The other branch of parliament is called the Seanad Éireann. Its 60 members are selected from representatives of education, agriculture, labor, industry, and public administration. The Seanad advises the prime minister and the Dáil.

Citizens who are at least 18 years old may vote. Local government is in the hands of 27 county councils and the five county boroughs of Dublin, Cork, Limerick, Galway, and Waterford. These councils are responsible for planning, taxing, and other local government activities.

Northern Ireland is part of the **United Kingdom**. But Northern Ireland has its own government. It is led by a first minister and a deputy minister. They are assisted by 10 ministers. Northern Ireland also has a parliament with 108 representatives.

In January 2000, Ireland's Prime Minister Bertie Ahern (L) and Northern Ireland's First Minister David Trimble met to discuss the progress of the 1998 peace agreement.

Holidays & Festivals

Many holidays and festivals take place around the country over the year. Since many Irish people are Catholic, they celebrate religious holidays like Easter, Epiphany, and All Saint's Day. St. Patrick's Day, March 17, is Ireland's national holiday. Dublin celebrates St. Patrick's day with a three-day festival and parade.

The Irish celebrate Christmas with family. Families usually go to a midnight **mass**. They also receive presents from Santa in their pillowcase. On December 26, or St. Stephen's day, groups of children dress up and sing hymns door to door.

Folk songs, dances, and traditional storytelling are featured at festivals that preserve Ireland's way of life. June 16 is Bloomsday in Dublin, celebrating James Joyce's novel, *Ulysses*. People hold reenactments and readings throughout the city. The Guinness Blues

Festival also takes place in Dublin. Famous musicians come from around the world to perform there.

In October, Cork has a film festival and Wexford has an opera festival. Galway Arts Festival takes place in July. It combines theater, music, and literary events.

Musicians play on the street at a traditional Irish festival.

Sports & Leisure

The most popular sports in Ireland are the traditional games of Gaelic football and **hurling**. Soccer, golf, and horse racing are also popular in Ireland.

The country has about 30 racetracks. Races are held throughout the year. Ireland holds the Irish Derby at Curragh Racecourse in July. The Irish Grand National is held near Dublin just after Easter. The Irish also enjoy horse shows, like the Royal Dublin Society Horse Show.

Most of the country's major museums and libraries are located in Dublin. These include the National Museum of Ireland, the National Gallery of Ireland, and the National Library of Ireland. The Royal Irish Academy is also in Dublin. The National Gallery, the Royal Hospital Kilmainham, and the Hugh Lane Municipal

Sports & Leisure

Children line up for pony games at the Royal Dublin Society Horse Show.

Girls prepare for an Irish dance.

Gallery of Modern Art in Dublin have large art collections.

There are opera seasons in Dublin and Cork. Ireland has several dance companies that perform often. Irish dancing is popular among adults and children. It can be seen at traditional Irish music festivals and at local events. The first Irish dancing show, *Riverdance*, is popular worldwide.

The Irish have a rich literary and artistic **heritage**. The late 1800s and early 1900s produced such great writers as William Butler Yeats, James Joyce,

George Augustus Moore, and Samuel Beckett. Irish poet Seamus Heaney won the 1995 **Nobel Prize for Literature**.

Irish theater is well established. In the 1990s, Irish directors and actors have had international fame. The Royal Hibernian Academy of Dublin has developed many Irish painters. Ireland's craftwork on jewelry and religious objects, such as Celtic crosses, reflects an ancient artistic tradition.

James Joyce

Glossary

bog - wet, spongy ground.

brew - to prepare beer or ale.

constitution - the laws that govern a country.

culture - the customs, arts, and tools of a nation or people at a certain time.

distill - to purify a liquid through a process of boiling and cooling.

economy - the way a state or nation uses its money, goods, and natural resources.

ferry - a boat that carries people and cargo across a body of water.

heritage - tradition.

hurling - a game resembling field hockey, with two teams of 15 players each.

mass - a worship ceremony in the Catholic Church.

mutton - meat from a sheep that is usually one to two years old.

Nobel Prize for Literature - an award for someone who has made outstanding accomplishments in literature.

parliament - the highest lawmaking body of some governments.

parliamentary democracy - a form of government in which the decisions of the nation are made by the people, through the elected body of parliament.

peat - a material formed by the remains of plants decaying in water.

pharmaceutical - of or relating to the industry that manufactures medicinal drugs.

stoat - a type of weasel native to Ireland.

United Kingdom - the united countries of England, Scotland, Wales, and Northern Ireland.

Web Sites

Embassy of Ireland in Washington, D.C.
http://www.irelandemb.org
Learn the latest news about Ireland, as well as basic information from economy to arts and culture.

About Ireland
http://www.irlgov.ie/aboutireland/Eng/default.asp
View photographs and learn more about life in Ireland on this page from the government of the Irish Republic.

The Irish Times
http://www.ireland.com
Learn about Ireland's current events, festivals, and culture at this site from one of Ireland's largest newspapers.

These sites are subject to change. Go to your favorite search engine and type in "Ireland" for more sites.

Index

A
Aer Lingus 26
Anglo-Irish Agreement 10
animals 16
art 4, 33, 34, 36, 37

B
Beckett, Samuel 37
Belfast 26

C
Celts 8, 18, 37
climate 14
communications 22, 23
Cork 24, 26, 30, 33, 36

D
Dáil Éireann 30
Dublin 24, 26, 30, 32, 33, 34, 36, 37

E
Easter Rising 10
economy 4, 10, 22, 24
education 18, 20
England 4, 8

F
farming 9, 22
festivals 32, 33
food 9, 20

G
Gaelic 18, 34
Galway 30, 33
geography 4, 12, 14, 24
government 4, 8, 10, 18, 22, 28, 30

H
Heaney, Seamus 37
holidays 32
housing 20

J
Joyce, James 32, 36

K
Knock 26

L
language 18, 26
Limerick 30
literature 32, 36, 37

M
Moore, George Augustus 37
museums 34
music 4, 32, 33, 36

N
Normans 8, 18
Northern Ireland 10, 12, 30

P
Patrick, Saint 8
plants 16
potato famine 9

R
religion 8, 18, 32
Riverdance 36

S
Seanad Éireann 30
Shannon 26
sports 34

T
theater 33, 37
transportation 26

U
Ulysses 32
Union, Act of 8
United Kingdom 8, 10, 30

V
Vikings 18

W
Waterford 30

Y
Yeats, William Butler 36

43355

941.5 Italia, Bob
Ita   Ireland

T 43355

BATTLE GROUND ACADEMY
Franklin, TN